For Miguel Estrada,
mi amigo del alma

WORLDVIEW GUIDE

The ODYSSEY

Dr. Louis Markos

canonpress
Moscow, Idaho

Published by Canon Press
P.O. Box 8729, Moscow, Idaho 83843
800.488.2034 | www.canonpress.com

Dr. Louis Markos, *Worldview Guide for the Odyssey*
Copyright © 2017 by Louis Markos.
For the Canon Classics edition of the epic (2017), go to www.canonpress.com/
books/canon-classics.

Cover design by James Engerbretson
Cover illustration by Forrest Dickison
Interior design by Valerie Anne Bost and James Engerbretson

Printed in the United States of America.

Library of Congress Cataloging-in-Publication Data
Markos, Louis, author.
Odyssey worldview guide / Louis Markos.
Moscow, Idaho : Canon Press, 2019.
LCCN 2019011341 | ISBN 9781944503918 (pbk. : alk. paper)
LCSH: Homer. Odyssey.
Classification: LCC PA4167 .M3545 2019 | DDC 883/.01—dc23
LC record available at https://lccn.loc.gov/2019011341

A free end-of-book test and answer key are available for download at
www.canonpress.com/ClassicsQuizzes

17 18 19 20 21 22   9 8 7 6 5 4 3 2 1

CONTENTS

INTRODUCTION

If the *Iliad* is the first tragedy ever written, then the *Odyssey* is the first comedy. Whereas the first gives us man the warrior, seeking glory on the battlefield, the second gives us man the husband and father, seeking domestic bliss with his family. The first values strength and prowess; the second wit and perseverance. The first takes place in a world where the dividing line between good and evil is often hard to identify; the second in a world where virtue and vice are more defined.

THE WORLD AROUND

There was almost surely a real war fought between the Greeks and the Trojans, whose city of Troy was located on the northwest coast of modern day Turkey. And that war was most likely fought around 1200 BC, at the height of the Mycenaean Bronze Age.

When we speak of the Mycenaeans, we speak of a loosely federated group of individual city-states spread out across Greece, but mostly located in the Peloponnese. The chief of these city-states was Mycenae, but there were others at Argos, Sparta, Pylos, Salamis, Phthia, Thebes, and Athens, not to mention the islands of Crete and Ithaca. The leader of each city-state was a king in his own right, though they all looked to Agamemnon of Mycenae as their commander-in-chief.

Although the Mycenaeans defeated the Trojans, they did not set up any bases in Troy; instead, they returned home with their plunder. But their glory and power was not to last much longer. By 1100, Mycenaean civilization had collapsed, plunging Greece into a three-hundred-year Dark Age during which the art of writing was lost.

In the absence of writing, an oral tradition sprang up to preserve the memory of the Golden Age of Mycenae. That oral tradition was later carried across the Aegean to the coast of modern day Turkey, where it was systematized and perfected by a group of bards who learned the skill of reciting long tales from memory.

Although the *Odyssey* takes place in the same time period as the *Iliad*, it offers us a world and an ethos that reflect the Dark Ages rather than the Mycenaean Bronze Age.

ABOUT THE AUTHOR

Though Homer was a Greek, he did not live in Greece but somewhere along the coast of Asia Minor (modern day Turkey). Seven cities competed for his birthplace, but he was most likely a resident of the island of Chios. Though we do not know for certain if Homer was blind, there is good reason to believe that he was—especially given the fact that he includes a blind bard in the *Odyssey* who may very well be a surrogate for himself.

The genius of Homer did not consist in his ability to "make up" stories out of his imagination, but to give shape to the oral tales of the homecomings (*nostoi* in Greek; root of our world nostalgia, which means "homecoming pain") of the Trojan warriors that had been handed down to him. It was most likely Homer who chose to center the *Odyssey* on Odysseus and his son Telemachus rather than on Agamemnon and Menelaus and their son/nephew Orestes.

Though he most likely lived near the end of the eighth century BC, at a time when Greece was reclaiming her written language from the Phoenicians, Homer was almost surely illiterate, the last in a long line of illiterate bards. The excessive use of repetition clearly identifies the epic as a product of oral composition.

If Homer did indeed write both the *Iliad* and *Odyssey*, and the full weight of ancient tradition says that he did, then he truly belongs in the category of Shakespeare. Whereas most great writers specialize in one specific genre and one defining mood, Homer, like Shakespeare, was equally adept at presenting tragedy (*Iliad*) and comedy (*Odyssey*) and at celebrating both war and peace, death and marriage.

WHAT OTHER
NOTABLES SAID

Traditionally, the *Iliad* is considered to be a greater, more epic work than the *Odyssey*. Written (probably) in the first century AD, Longinus's influential treatise "On the Sublime" expresses this view: the *Iliad* "was written at the height of [Homer's] inspiration, full of action and conflict, while the *Odyssey* for the most part consists of narrative, as is characteristic of old age. Accordingly, in the *Odyssey*, Homer may be likened to a sinking sun, whose grandeur remains without its intensity. He does not in the *Odyssey* maintain so high a pitch as in those poems of Ilium. His sublimities are not evenly sustained and free from the liability to sink; there is not the same profusion of accumulated passions, nor the supple and oratorical style, packed with images drawn from real life."[1]

---

1. Longinus, *On the Sublime*, in *Critical Theory Since Plato*, rev. edition, ed. by Hazard Adams (New York: HBJ, 1992), 81.

Still, most readers today would give first place to the *Odyssey* on account of its masterful storytelling and its more memorable and relatable characters. Greco-Roman historian Michael Grant, partly playing off the Longinus quote above, lists the differences in the *Odyssey* that have made it the more popular of the two epics:

> The *Odyssey*, like the *Iliad*, is a display of courage, endurance and resourcefulness. But it is much more complex in structure—an epic changing into a novel . . . Mind and character now prevail over circumstances . . . Love of wife and home has started to take precedence over love of comrades and honor, and courtliness over chivalry. . . while there is less deep and tragic feeling than in the *Iliad*, there is emphasis on hospitality, friendship, acquired courtesy, and the forms and formalities of decorum; the story of Telemachus is the story of the education of a hero within this framework.[2]

The *Odyssey* has also had an even greater impact on popular culture than its predecessor. The word "Odyssey" itself means a great adventure (e.g., *2001: A Space Odyssey*) and it has been loosely adapted by the Coen Brothers' film, *O Brother Where Art Thou*? James Joyce's *Ulysses* teases its readers with constant allusions to the classic, and even the children's story *Watership Down* borrows themes from it.

---

2. Michael Grant, *Myths of the Greeks and Romans* (New York: New American Library, 1962), 76-77.

PLOT SUMMARY, SETTING, AND CHARACTERS

- *Setting: Various islands in the Mediterranean and then the island of Ithaca off the west coast of Greece, around 1200 BC.*
- *Odysseus:* Son of Laertes, King of Ithaca, Sacker of Cities, Master of Stratagems
- *Penelope:* Faithful wife of Odysseus who shares her husband's wit
- *Telemachus:* Son of Odysseus who proves to be both brave and courteous
- *Athena:* Daughter of Zeus and goddess of wisdom/war; patron of Odysseus
- *Hermes:* Son of Zeus and messenger of the gods who helps Odysseus
- *Poseidon:* God of the Sea; Odysseus's foe throughout the epic

- *Polyphemus:* Cyclops son of Poseidon; he prays to his father to curse Odysseus
- *Menelaus:* Brother of Agamemnon, King of Sparta, husband of Helen
- *Nestor:* King of Pylos whose son, Peisistratus, travels with Telemachus
- *Antinous* and *Eurymachus:* Two head suitors on Ithaca
- *Eumaeus* and *Eurycleia:* Faithful swineherd and nurse on Ithaca
- *Lotus Eaters:* Seemingly hospitable islanders who addict guests to their honey-sweet lotus, making them forget their homes
- *Aeolus:* God of the Wind who puts all the bad winds in a bag to help Odysseus
- *Laestrygonians:* Man-eating giants who destroy all but one of Odysseus's ships
- *Circe:* Enchantress who turns men to swine but is defeated by Odysseus
- *Tiresias:* Blind prophet whom Odysseus meets in the underworld
- *Agamemnon:* King of Mycenae who is killed by Aegisthus, the lover of his wife, Clytemnestra; his son, Orestes, later avenges him by killing Aegisthus
- *Achilles:* Greatest of the Greek warriors whom Odysseus meets in the underworld

- *Sirens:* Bird-women creatures who lure sailors to the rocks with their song
- *Scylla* and *Charybdis:* A beast with six heads and a giant whirlpool between which sailors have to navigate; whichever they choose, they risk much
- *Calypso:* Lovely goddess who offers to make Odysseus immortal
- *Nausicaa:* Princess of Phaeacia, takes in Odysseus when he washes up on shore
- *Alcinous* and *Arete:* King and Queen of Phaeacia, parents of Nausicaa

The *Odyssey* tells the story of Odysseus's ten-year journey from Troy back to his island home of Ithaca. It begins, like the *Iliad*, not at the beginning of the story but *in medias res* (Latin for "in the middle of things"), during the final year of his wanderings.

Books I–IV introduce Odysseus's son, Telemachus, as he waits disconsolately for the return of his father. Athena appears to rouse him to action, instructing him to visit Nestor and Menelaus to find out if his father is still alive. Meanwhile a group of evil suitors press Penelope to marry one of them.

Taking place simultaneously with Books I–IV, Books V–VIII reveal that Odysseus has been stranded on Calypso's island for seven years (*Calypso* is Greek for "hidden"). But Zeus sends Hermes to Calypso to tell her to release Odysseus. Odysseus leaves on a raft but is wrecked by

Poseidon and washes ashore on Phaeacia, where Nausicaa helps him. The Phaeacians graciously agree to take Odysseus back to Ithaca, but first he tells them of his journeys.

Books IX–XII tell in flashback and in first person how Odysseus eluded the Lotus Eaters and defeated the cannibalistic Cyclops Polyphemus by getting him drunk and putting out his eye. Unfortunately, as Odysseus escaped, he boasted of his triumph, allowing Polyphemus, son of Poseidon, to curse him, causing him to arrive late in Ithaca having lost all his men and finding his home in turmoil.

The curse set in as members of Odysseus's crew 1) opened up a bag of wind that had been given him by the hospitable Aeolus, causing them to be blown off course; 2) got eaten by the giant Laestrygonians; and 3) were turned to swine by Circe the enchantress. Though Odysseus survived, he had to visit the underworld for information about how to avoid such monsters as the sirens and Scylla and Charybdis. Finally, when his surviving men ate the forbidden Cattle of the Sun, they were all killed, leaving Odysseus alone and stranded on the island of Calypso.

After the sympathetic Phaeacians set him back home on Ithaca (Books XIII-XXIV), Odysseus reveals himself to Telemachus and the two plot together, first to test and then to kill the evil suitors. Husband and wife are reunited, and order is restored.

WORLDVIEW ANALYSIS

The reader who moves from the *Iliad* to the *Odyssey* should notice immediately that the *Odyssey* takes place in a far more ethical world where the distinctions between good and evil are clearer for both the characters and the reader. Whereas we feel great remorse when Hector, the purported antagonist of the *Iliad*, dies, we feel no sorrow whatsoever when Odysseus kills the suitors.

In the last book of the *Iliad*, Achilles says that Zeus has two urns by his throne: one filled with blessings; the other with curses. When he showers on us the contents of the first, our lives are filled with joy; when the contents of the second rain down on us, our lives are destroyed by suffering and pain. How does Zeus choose which urn to draw from? No one can say; at least from Achilles' point of view, the choice is arbitrary.

In the first book of the *Odyssey*, Zeus himself rejects this point of view: "What a lamentable thing it is that men should blame the gods and regard *us* as the source of their troubles, when it is their own transgressions which bring them suffering that was not their destiny" (I.32–25).[3] Then, to prove his point, he tells the melodramatic story of how Agamemnon was killed by Aegisthus, the lover of his wife, Clytemnestra. Aegisthus was wrong to do this deed, asserts Zeus, and was justly killed by Agamemnon's son, Orestes.

It is safe to suggest that Homer here agrees with Zeus, for, in telling the story of the family of Agamemnon, he leaves out those parts that muddy the ethical waters. Thus, in the fuller version of the story—later dramatized by the Greek tragedian Aeschylus in his trilogy, the *Oresteia*—Agamemnon is killed by his wife (not by her lover), and Orestes follows his slaying of Aegisthus by doing the same to his mother. Matricide and wives-killing-husbands make for great tragic dilemmas, but that is not Homer's focus.

To drive home the ethical worldview around which his epic is constructed, Homer skillfully parallels the Agamemnon-Clytemnestra-Aegisthus-Orestes subplot with his central story of Odysseus, Penelope, the suitors, and Telemachus. The suitors, like Aegisthus, are simple villains, and no taboos are broken when Telemachus, like Orestes, avenges the indignities paid to his father.

---

3. All quotes from Homer are taken from *The Odyssey*, trans. by E. V. Rieu, rev. by D. C. H. Rieu (London: Penguin, 1991). References from this prose translation will be given in the text by book and line number.

(Telemachus, in fact, consciously takes up Orestes as his role model.) That Penelope, *unlike* Clytemnestra, stays faithful to her absent husband only emphasizes further that our choices determine our fate.

Since the *Odyssey* takes place in a moral universe, it is vital that readers be provided with a key for distinguishing the good guys from the bad guys. In the Bible, the virtues of obedience, gratitude, faith, hope, and love separate saint from sinner, the righteous from the unrighteous. In the *Odyssey*, it is the good relationship between the guest and the host (*xenia* in Greek) that distinguishes the hero from the villain.

We immediately know Telemachus is a good person, for, when Athena comes to the palace in disguise, Telemachus alone takes her in and feeds her. While visiting Nestor and Menelaus, he further reveals his *xenia* by being a good and noble guest. The suitors, on the other hand, are bad guests who take advantage of Penelope's hospitality, just as the Lotus Eaters and Calypso are bad hosts who detain their guests against their will.

While on his journeys, Odysseus meets both good hosts (Aeolus, who freely gives him a bag of wind that will afford him safe passage home; the Phaeacians, who feed him royally and then escort him back to Ithaca) and bad hosts (Polyphemus, who, rather than feeding Odysseus's men, feeds *on* them; Circe, who turns his men to swine). In most cases, Odysseus is a good guest; however, in the cave of Polyphemus, Odysseus plays the role of a bad guest and pays for it by provoking the Cyclops' curse.

Though *xenia* is not as strong a theme in the Bible, hospitality is significant in the Old Testament—where the men of Sodom and Gomorrah are punished for treating the angels who visit their town with contempt and perverse lust (Genesis 19)—and in the New—where we are instructed to show hospitality because, by so doing, we may entertain angels unawares (Heb. 13:2). Whether in the Bible or in the *Odyssey*, the way one treats a guest or a host offers a window into that person's soul, revealing his inner character.

Though Odysseus is the protagonist of the epic, Homer unexpectedly devotes Books I–IV to Telemachus' maturation process. Like so many characters in literature (Orestes, Henry V, Huck Finn, Frodo Baggins) and the Bible (Samuel, David, Peter, Paul) Telemachus must go through a rite of passage that will test his mettle and enable him to come of age.

In Telemachus' case, he must discover whether he is the true son of his father. In the epic, it is Athena who calls upon the unsure, untested Telemachus to live up to his noble father: "You are no longer a child: you must put childish thoughts away. . . . You, my friend—and what a tall and splendid young man you have grown!—must be as brave as Orestes. Then future generations will sing your praises" (I.297–304; see 1 Cor. 13:11 for an interesting, though probably unconscious, echo by the classically educated Paul).

Whereas the typical teenager of today would balk at being told to live up to the deeds of some other young man, much less the deeds of his father, Telemachus eagerly accepts the challenge. Like a biblical hero, but unlike most modern heroes, Telemachus realizes that he lives and acts within a web of duties, responsibilities, and familial relationships which he cannot simply throw off. He is the son of Odysseus, not one of the *xenia*-despising suitors.

On the same day, somewhere on the other side of the Mediterranean, Odysseus, too, makes the choice to be true to his duties and familial identity. When Calypso, desperate to convince Odysseus to remain with her and accept her gift of immortality, expresses doubt that Penelope can exceed her in beauty, Odysseus freely admits that "my wise Penelope's looks and stature are insignificant compared with yours. For she is mortal, while you have immortality and unfading youth. Nevertheless I long to reach my home and see the day of my return. It is my never-failing wish" (V.216–221).

There is a wealth of wisdom and insight in that word "nevertheless" that cuts to the core of what it means to be human. If he is not the husband of Penelope, the son of Telemachus, and the King of Ithaca, then he is not really Odysseus. When most people today hear the name Odysseus, they think of someone with a wanderlust who wants to sail the seven seas (in great part because he is depicted that way in Alfred, Lord Tennyson's stirring Victorian poem, "Ulysses"), but that is not the Odysseus of Homer. His hero desires only one thing: to return home.

To say that Odysseus is a Greek Sinbad the Sailor is tantamount to saying that Paul traveled across the Mediterranean world because he was a tourist. Paul's travels had only one end: to spread the gospel. Just so, Odysseus travels only so that he may be reunited with his family. That is not to say he is a Christian hero. Like Jacob, he is not above being a deceiver and a trickster; like David, his sexual ethics are decidedly suspect. He also delays far longer than he should on the island of Circe, almost succumbing to the false homecoming that Circe tempts him with.

Nevertheless, he possesses an integrity that allows him to remain whole. Only in the cave of the Cyclops, when he misuses his identity and boastfully shouts out his name to Polyphemus, does he suffer a loss of that integrity—a loss that carries with it terrible consequences. After that slip, however, he grows increasingly in his self-understanding, and is even able to bear up under the numinous dread of visiting Hades and facing his own eventual death. Indeed, when he turns down Calypso's offer of immortality to return home to Penelope, he does so *after* he has seen how dreary the afterlife is. Still, he chooses to be mortal, for that is who and what he is.

Odysseus's moral growth, seen so powerfully in his refusal of immortality and of the suitor-like *luxuria* that Circe, Calypso, and Nausicaa offer, is also evidenced in

Book IX, when he freely confesses to the Phaeacians his own guilt in provoking the Cyclops to wrath. Even though he must practice trickery on Ithaca to survive and exact his just revenge on the suitors, he has learned the value of honesty and that there are people, like the Phaeacians, who can and should be trusted.

In its moral-ethical outlook, the *Odyssey* overlaps with some key aspects of the Judeo-Christian worldview; however, it is in its overall narrative thrust that Homer's epic most closely parallels the story of scripture. Both the *Odyssey* and the Bible hinge upon the promised messianic coming of a good king who will restore justice by punishing the wicked and exalting the faithful. Our world, like Homer's Ithaca, is trapped in a state of futility from which it cannot free itself; it needs the intervention of a savior-judge who will arrive in the fullness of time and set things to right.

Although Books I–XII, which chronicle the dual journeys of Odysseus and his son, move swiftly, Books XIII–XXIV, during which Odysseus takes back his home, are often gruelingly slow-paced. But that slowness—which itself mimics the gradual unfolding of God's plan for human history—is used to draw out three themes that are also central to the Bible: recognition, endurance, and discernment.

Rather than announce his arrival the moment he lands on the beach of Ithaca, Odysseus, guided by Athena, only reveals himself to those he can trust. Not everyone on the island desires to see the return of the true king, and so he must be cautious, only revealing himself to those who have eyes to see and ears to hear.

In what may be the best known and most beloved moments in the epic, Odysseus, who wears a disguise throughout most of the second half of the epic, is only recognized by his faithful dog, Argus, who lifts his head at the approach of his master and then dies peacefully. Even so, when the Son of God came into the world as a mortal man, there were precious few who recognized him. To his own people the Messiah came, John sadly informs us in his prologue, but they neither knew nor accepted him (Jn. 1:10–11).

As the Son of God took the form of a poor servant from whom men turned their faces (see Is. 53:2–3), so Odysseus is disguised by Athena as an old and dirty beggar from whom most of the Ithacans turn in scorn. Of all his trials and tribulations, this proves to be the hardest for him, for he must bear up under humiliating indignities, even though he is the rightful king come home to his palace and his throne. He even has stools hurled at his head by the worst of the suitors. Still, as Christ will do over a thousand years later, he endures the scorn for the greater prize that awaits him (Heb. 12:2).

By suffering the suitor's insults, Odysseus is made a more perfect and obedient deliverer (see Heb. 5:7–10); but he also is empowered to do something of great importance. He is put in a position to test the suitors one by one so as to discern which of them is wholly evil and which can yet be redeemed. In a line that, like so many verses in the Bible, combines free will with the sovereign choice of God, Homer has Athena urge the disguised Odysseus "to go round collecting scraps from the Suitors and so learn to distinguish the good from the bad, though this did not mean that in the end she was to save a single one from destruction" (XVII.361–364).

Because of this careful sifting of the wheat from the chaff, when Odysseus brings down Armageddon on the evil suitors, both he and we are assured of the justice of his actions. In fact, when Eurycleia, Odysseus's faithful nurse, begins to gloat over the death of the suitors, Odysseus stops her, saying, "Restrain yourself, old woman, and gloat in silence. I'll have no cries of triumph here. It is an impious thing to exult over the slain. These men fell victims to the will of the gods and their own infamy. They paid respect to no one on earth who came near them—good or bad. And now their own transgressions have brought them to this ignominious death" (XXII.410–416).

QUOTABLES

1. "The goddess spoke and the next moment she was
   gone, vanishing like a bird through a hole in the roof.
   In Telemachus' heart she had implanted spirit and
   daring, and had brought the image of his father to
   his mind even more strongly than before. He felt the
   change and was overcome with awe, for he realized
   a god had been with him. Then, godlike himself, he
   rejoined the Suitors."
   ~ the effect Athena has on Telemachus (I.319–324)

2. "And may the gods grant you your heart's desire; may
   they give you a husband and a home, and the blessing
   of harmony so much to be desired, since there is noth-
   ing better or finer than when two people of one heart
   and mind keep house as man and wife, a grief to their

enemies and a joy to their friends, and their reputation
spreads far and wide."

~ *Odysseus to Nausicaa expressing the good life in this
epic* (VI.18–186)

3. "Now these natives had no intention of killing my
    comrades; what they did was to give them some lotus
    to taste. Those who ate the honeyed fruit of the plant
    lost any wish to come back and bring us news. All
    they now wanted was to stay where they were with the
    Lotus-eaters, to browse on the lotus, and to forget all
    thoughts of return. I had to use force to bring them
    back to the hollow ships, and they wept on the way, but
    once on board I tied them up and dragged them under
    the benches."

    ~ *the effect of the lotus on Odysseus's men* (IX.92–99)

4. "And do not you make light of death, illustrious
    Odysseus. . . . I would rather work the soil as a serf on
    hire to some landless impoverished peasant than be
    King of all these lifeless dead."

    ~ *Achilles to Odysseus on the dreariness of Hades*
    (XI.487–490)

5. "Draw near, illustrious Odysseus, man of many tales,
    great glory of the Achaeans, and bring your ship to rest
    so that you may hear our voices. No seaman ever sailed
    his black ship past this spot without listening to the
    honey-sweet tones that flow from our lips, and no one
    who has listened has not been delighted and gone on

his way a wiser man. For we know all that the Argives and Trojans suffered on the broad plain of Troy by the will of the gods, and we know whatever happens on this fruitful earth."

~ *the song of the Sirens* (XII.184–191)

21 SIGNIFICANT QUESTIONS AND ANSWERS

1. Why does Homer choose to begin his epic in the final year of Odysseus's wanderings rather than with the fall of Troy?

    As with the *Iliad*, Homer does not begin his epic *ab ovo* (Latin for "from the egg"), but plunges *in medias res* (Latin for "in the middle of things"), thus starting his epic at a moment of great tension. By holding off the beginning, Homer also gives Telemachus time to grow up—that's why Odysseus must spend seven years hidden away with Calypso (*Calypso* means "hidden" in Greek). This narrative device allows Homer to chart the dual journey and maturation process of father and son.

2. How does the narrative structure of the *Odyssey* differ from that of the *Iliad*?

In a fashion that is surprisingly modern, Homer
offers us parallel action in Books I-IV (the journey
of Telemachus) and Books V-VIII (the journey of
Odysseus). Books IX-XII are then told in flashback, narrating what happened in the nine years
leading up to Book I. Because Books IX-XII are
told in flashback, we get to hear Odysseus speak in
first person, thus making him appear to be a real
historical character.

3. What did ancient critics say about Books I-IV?

Ancient critics considered Books I-IV to be a
sort of mini-epic, focusing on the son of the great
hero. They even gave that mini-epic a name: the
Telemachia. In the third-century BC, Apollonius of
Rhodes, one of the chief librarians of the Library of
Alexandria, wrote his own four-book epic on Jason's
Quest for the Golden Fleece, the *Argonautica*
(Greek for "Voyage of the Argo," Jason's ship).

4. Why does Telemachus have to visit Nestor and
Menelaus?

The official reason why Telemachus must visit his
father's comrades from the Trojan War is to obtain
information from them about Odysseus's where-
abouts. But there is another reason he must go.
If Telemachus is to fight, and perhaps die, for his
home, then he must first see what a working home
looks like. The good life in the *Odyssey* is domestic
rather than military, and it is vital that Telemachus

see what that life can be like before he fights the
suitors to attain it.

5. How does Penelope hold off the suitors for so many
    years?

> Though Penelope does not possess the physical
> strength of her husband, she shares his wit. Rather
> than wield a sword, she wields her feminine skill
> for working at the loom. She tells the suitors that
> she cannot marry one of them until she weaves a
> burial shroud for her father-in-law, Laertes. After
> they agree, she proceeds to weave the loom in full
> view of the suitors by day, but then undoes her work
> each night. By this stratagem, she holds them off
> for three years.

6. How exactly should the guest-host relationship (*xenia*)
    work?

> According to the rules of *xenia*, when a stranger
> comes to your door, you must take him in and feed
> him *before* asking his name. Only after taking care
> of his needs may you ask his name and story. The
> guest, on the other hand, is obliged to treat his
> host's property with respect and not overstay his
> welcome. Polyphemus, the archetypal bad host, *first*
> asks the names of his visitors and then eats them.

7. Why does Athena, and other gods, appear in disguise
    most of the time?

Although the *Odyssey* is a more ethical poem than
the *Iliad*, it takes place in a world where things are
less certain and where treachery has grown. The
gods are farther away and do not speak as directly
as they did in the *Iliad*. Incidentally, Athena takes
on the guise of a man named Mentor in order
to guide Telemachus on his journey; it is for that
reason that people today who take a young person
under their wing in order to teach and direct him
are called mentors.

8. What qualities does a hero need to survive and thrive
in the world of the *Odyssey*?

In the *Iliad*, it is enough for a warrior to be strong
and fearless. In the *Odyssey*, he must also possess a
gracious tongue and be wise and discerning in his
speech. Like the later knights of King Arthur, he
must be both brave and courteous. In addition, he
must have the ability to look through disguises and
deceptions; he must not be fooled by appearances,
but must persevere until the truth is revealed.

9. Can you give an example of someone holding on
through disguises to reach the truth?

Menelaus shares with Telemachus an adventure he
had on the coast of Egypt. In order to obtain the
information he needs to get home, he is told that
he must capture and hold down Proteus, the Old
Man of the Sea. Menelaus is warned that when he
holds down Proteus, he will change his shape from

one form to another to frighten him; but that if he holds Proteus firmly until he returns to his original form, then Menelaus will be able to ask him questions and receive the answers he needs.

10. What are the two types of dangers Odysseus faces on his journeys?

The first type of danger Odysseus faces are threats to his life from savage beasts like the Cyclops, the Laestrygonians, and Scylla and Charybdis. To survive these dangers, Odysseus must draw on both his courage and his cleverness. The second type of danger is a more subtle one: that of being seduced by a false homecoming. Circe, Calypso, and Nausicaa all promise to provide the travel-weary hero with a surrogate Penelope and a new Ithaca. But Odysseus presses on through these false Penelopes until he is reunited with the real one.

11. What is the lure of the Sirens that makes them so dangerous?

In modern books and films, a Siren is usually depicted as a beautiful but cold blonde who seduces men and lures them to their doom. But the Sirens in the *Odyssey* are not beautiful; they are not even women. They have the faces and torsos of women, but the bodies of birds. It is their beautiful voices that lure sailors to the rocks; yet, even here, there is a frequent misunderstanding. Their lovely songs do not promise sex but knowledge of all things on

the earth. Odysseus succeeds in hearing their voices
without being killed by stuffing his men's ears with
wax and having them tie him to the mast.

12. What does it mean to navigate between Scylla and Charybdis?

In the *Odyssey*, Scylla and Charybdis face each
other across the narrow Strait of Messina that runs
between Italy and Sicily. The former, a six-headed
beast, lives in a high cave; when ships pass, she ex-
tends her doglike mouths and devours one sailor in
each mouth. The latter lives in an underwater cave
and periodically sucks in all the water in the strait,
causing a whirlpool. To navigate between the two is
to make a choice where either option threatens di-
saster. Scylla and Charybdis may also lie behind the
phrase "caught between a rock and a hard place."

13. Why must Odysseus travel into the underworld?

According to Circe, Odysseus must travel to
Hades so that he can meet the shade of the blind
prophet Tiresias and receive advice that he will
need to make it safely home. But there must be
more to it than that, for nearly everything Tiresias
tells Odysseus is later told to him again by Circe.
Odysseus's descent into the underworld (*nekuia*
in Greek) is meant to test the hero's courage and
endurance in the face of his own mortality. So influential was this scene in western literature that the

nekuia became a standard literary convention used by Virgil, Dante, and Milton.

14. Why does Homer give so prominent a role to Eumaeus the swineherd?

Homer was clearly fond of Eumaeus, whom he refers to as a prince among swineherds. Through his character, we see that servants can be as noble and heroic as their masters, and that loyalty is one of the greatest of virtues. Eumaeus, a curmudgeon with a heart of gold, has been a surrogate father for Telemachus in Odysseus's absence; he has steered him away from the vices of the suitors.

15. How does Penelope show her faithfulness in the *Odyssey*?

Penelope shows her faithfulness in two ways. First, she uses her wits to hold off the suitors, remaining loyal to her absent husband and her young son. Second, she calls for a contest and pledges to marry the winner. The reason she does this is not because she wants to marry one of the suitors (the thought disgusts her) but because she had promised Odysseus that if he did not return by the time her son had become a young man, she would marry again. By staying true to her promise, she sets in motion the contest that allows Odysseus to defeat the suitors.

16. How does Odysseus differ from and resemble the
    heroes of the Bible?

> The heroes of the Bible begin in weakness and are
> made strong by God's aid; Odysseus, on the other
> hand, is strong and clever to begin with—traits
> which convince Athena to jump on his already
> winning team. Still, like the patriarchs of the Old
> Testament and the apostles of the New, Odysseus
> must trust for many years to the road. By doing so,
> he set a literary precedent that has been repeated
> in countless literary works: *Aeneid*, *Divine Comedy*,
> *Canterbury Tales*, *Don Quixote*, *Pilgrim's Progress*,
> *The Grapes of Wrath*, *Moby-Dick*, *The Lord of the
> Rings*, etc.

17. Why does Homer build a friendship between
    Telemachus and Peisistratus?

> Though no explanation is given for why Homer
> matches Telemachus up with Nestor's son
> Peisistratus, I would give two reasons. First,
> Peisistratus represents, in sharp contrast to the
> young suitors, the right kind of friend that
> Telemachus needs if he is to mature into a good
> young man. Second, it is very possible that the
> *Odyssey* was put into written form under the
> auspices of the sixth-century BC Athenian tyrant,
> Peisistratus; perhaps this character was added then
> to flatter him.

18. How does Odysseus win back Penelope and why is that significant?

> Odysseus wins back his wife by being the only person strong enough and skilled enough to string his bow and shoot an arrow through a difficult target. It is significant that the bow Odysseus strings is not one that he brought with him to Troy but which he only used for hunting on his estate. In that sense, the bow represents the domestic sphere rather than the battlefield.

19. Why is Odysseus so cruel to the maids and serving women?

> Though most readers feel little remorse for the suitors slain by Odysseus and Telemachus, many are disturbed that Odysseus hangs the female lovers of the suitors. Given that Odysseus has sex with both Circe and Calypso, it might seem that he is being hypocritical in killing the maids for their illicit affairs. But his reason for doing so would be clear to Homer's audience. The maids have sullied their mistresses' home, bringing shame and scandal; as such, they are as much traitors as the suitors. That is why Eurycleia supports their execution.

20. How is Odysseus able to convince Penelope that he has truly returned home?

> Afraid that she will be fooled by a false Odysseus and end up, like Helen of Troy, unfaithful to her husband, Penelope is suspicious when the beggar

claims to be Odysseus. To test whether or not he is who he claims to be, she instructs the servants to drag her bed out of the bedroom so that the beggar can sleep in the hallway. Immediately, Odysseus, who carved their marriage bed out of the top of a single tree and thus knows that it cannot be moved, exclaims that such a thing would be impossible. When Penelope hears this, she knows that the man is Odysseus, for only he, a single servant, and she herself know the secret of the bed.

21. In Book XXIV, Homer gives us a final glimpse of the underworld, where we hear Agamemnon describe the funeral of Achilles and the dead suitors tell of their death at the hands of Odysseus. Why does Homer include this seemingly anti-climactic scene?

> Though Homer does not give an explanation for why he includes this strange scene, I believe that he does so as a way of rounding off both the *Iliad* and *Odyssey*. Whereas Achilles achieves the good reward of the Iliadic hero (dying a soldier's death and receiving a grand funeral) and Odysseus achieves the good reward of the Odyssean hero (reunion with his family), Agamemnon (who was murdered by his wife's lover) gets neither.

FURTHER DISCUSSION AND REVIEW

Master what you have read by reviewing and integrating the different elements of this classic.

SETTING AND CHARACTERS
Be able to compare and contrast the personalities (including strengths, weaknesses, and mannerisms) of each character. How does the setting affect the characters?

PLOT
Be able to describe the beginning, middle, and end of the book along with specific details that move the plot forward and make it compelling. This includes the success or downfall (or both) of each character.

CONFLICT
Go through the character list and describe the tension between any and all main characters. Then, think about

whether any characters have internal conflict (in their own minds). What is the significance of the overt conflict (fighting) or any conflict with impersonal forces?

THEME STATEMENTS

Be able to describe what this classic is telling us about the world. Is the message true? What truth can we take from the plot, characters, conflict, and themes (even if the author didn't believe that truth)? Do any objects take on added meaning because of repetition or their place in the story (i.e., do any objects become symbols)? Be able to explain the following themes (or any others you've noticed) in this classic:

> In a world where a meal is hard to come by (and where pirates or monsters could easily harm you), a proper guest-host relationship (*xenia*) is of the utmost importance. In the *Odyssey*, you can judge a man (or monster) by how he treats his guests.

> Throughout their journey, Odysseus and his friends are presented with false homecomings that promise safety, security, and an easy life in exchange for the endurance, pain, and wit that are required of a great hero.

> Whereas excessive boasting and complacent over-confidence destroy, a man needs to use disguises and deceptions to achieve lasting success.

Finally, compose your own theme statement about some element, large or small, of this classic. Then, use the Bible and common sense to assess the truth of that theme statement. Identify your own key words or borrow from the following list as a starting point: *faithfulness and endurance*; *courteous speech*; *family relationships*; *fate and choice*; *coming of age*; *revenge vs. justice*; *reconciliation*.

A NOTE FROM THE PUBLISHER:
TAKING THE CLASSICS QUIZ

Once you have finished the worldview guide, you can prepare for the end-of-book test. Each test will consist of a short-answer section on the book itself and the author, a short-answer section on plot and the narrative, and a long-answer essay section on worldview, conflict, and themes.

Each quiz, along with other helps, can be downloaded for free at www.canonpress.com/ClassicsQuizzes. If you have any questions about the quiz or its answers or the Worldview Guides in general, you can contact Canon Press at service@canonpress.com or 208.892.8074.

Dr. Louis Markos is a Professor of English and holds the Robert H. Ray Chair in Humanities at Houston Baptist University. He has written books such as *From Achilles to Christ*, *Lewis Agonistes*, *Apologetics for the 21st Century*, *On the Shoulders of Hobbits*, and many other books on classics, romantic poetry, and C.S. Lewis. He has written for *Christianity Today*, *Touchstone*, *Christian Research Journal*, *Christian Scholar's Review*, and many others. His modern adaptations of Euripides' *Iphigenia in Tauris*, Euripides' *Helen*, and Sophocles' *Electra* have been performed off-Broadway. He has also written a children's novel, *The Dreaming Stone*, in which his kids become part of Greek mythology. In the sequel, *In the Shadow of Troy*, they become part of the *Iliad* and *Odyssey*.